Marks and Spencer p.l.c.
Baker Street, London, W1U 8EP

www.marksandspencer.com

Copyright © Exclusive Editions 2003

ISBN: 1-84273-925-5

Printed in China

Produced by the Bridgewater Book Company Ltd.

Photographer Calvey Taylor-Haw

Home Economist Ruth Pollock

NOTES FOR THE READER

- This book uses both metric and imperial measurements. Follow the same units of measurement throughout; do not mix metric and imperial.

- All spoon measurements are level: teaspoons are assumed to be 5 ml, and tablespoons are assumed to be 15 ml.

- Unless otherwise stated, milk is assumed to be full fat and eggs are medium.

- Recipes using raw or very lightly cooked eggs should be avoided by infants, the elderly, pregnant women, convalescents and anyone suffering from an illness.

- Optional ingredients, variations or serving suggestions have not been included in the calculations. The times given are an approximate guide only. Preparation times differ according to the techniques used by different people and the cooking times may also vary from those given.

contents

introduction

Curried dishes have become hugely popular with Westerners in recent years. As their popularity has spread, some of the classic recipes have been adapted to accommodate the tastes of other cultures, or new recipes have been invented. In Britain, for example, the traditional Indian rice and lentil dish known as kedgeree is now a breakfast dish that contains fish. Chicken tikka masala was actually created in Britain in a Bangladeshi restaurant, and not in India as many people believe.

In this book you will find a large selection of curries, not just from India but from other parts of the world too, such as Thailand and the Caribbean. They range from irresistible poultry and meat dishes such as Chicken Jalfrezi and Lamb Do Piaza, to exciting fish and seafood dishes including Monkfish & Coconut Curry and Seafood Laksa. There is also a chapter devoted to delicious side dishes, including Asian Coconut Rice, Naan Breads and Lime Pickle. Vegetarians need not feel left out; this book features a wealth of mouthwatering meatless dishes, which will tempt vegetarians and meat-eaters alike. From a Spicy Dhal or a Vegetable Korma, to Vegetable Samosas and Onion Bhajis, there is sure to be something here to satisfy all tastes.

guide to recipe key		
	easy	Recipes are graded as follows: 1 pea = easy; 2 peas = very easy; 3 peas = extremely easy.
	serves 4	Recipes generally serve four people. Simply halve the ingredients to serve two, taking care not to mix imperial and metric measurements.
	10 minutes	Preparation time. Where marinating or soaking are involved, these times have been added on separately: e.g. 15 minutes + 30 minutes to marinate.
	10 minutes	Cooking time. Cooking times don't include the cooking of side dishes or accompaniments served with the main dishes.

chicken korma
page 14

seafood laksa
page 44

thai green curry
page 64

naan breads
page 84

poultry & meat

In this chapter you will find some of the most well-known and best-loved curries, from a luxurious Chicken Tikka and a delicious Rogan Josh, to a satisfying Pork Vindaloo. For something a little different, sample the fragrant Green Duck Curry or the rich Indonesian Beef Curry. If you want to create a less fiery dish, try cutting down on the quantities of spices, or remove the seeds from fresh chillies where included. You can also ring the changes by replacing the chicken with turkey in some recipes or experimenting with your own blends of aromatic herbs and spices.

chicken tikka

		ingredients	
very easy		450 g/1 lb skinless, boneless chicken breasts, cut into bite-sized chunks	1½ tsp chilli powder
		1 tsp salt	1 tsp garam masala
serves 4		5 tbsp lemon juice	1 tsp turmeric
		4–6 tbsp single cream	1 tsp paprika
15 minutes + 2–8 hours to marinate		MARINADE	1 tsp ground coriander
		1 large garlic clove, finely chopped	2 tsp chopped fresh coriander
		½ onion, grated	100 ml/3½ fl oz natural yogurt
		1 tbsp desiccated coconut	freshly ground black pepper, to taste
15 minutes		1 tsp ground cumin	sprigs of fresh coriander, to garnish lemon wedges, to serve

Put the chicken, salt and lemon juice into a non-metallic bowl and mix together well. In a separate bowl, mix all the marinade ingredients together, then add to the chicken and stir gently to combine. Cover with clingfilm and refrigerate for at least 2 hours, or preferably overnight.

When ready to cook, remove from the refrigerator, then thread the chicken pieces on to skewers and baste with some of the marinade. Barbecue over hot coals or cook under a preheated hot grill for 15 minutes, turning and basting frequently with the remaining marinade.

Remove the chicken skewers from the heat, transfer to a serving platter and pour over the cream. Garnish with coriander sprigs and serve with lemon wedges.

chicken madras

		ingredients	
	very easy	1 tsp ground ginger	2 large onions, chopped
		1½ tsp turmeric	1 tbsp lemon juice
	serves 4	1 tsp ground cumin	2 tsp tomato purée
		1 tsp garam masala	few drops of red food colouring
		2 tsp chilli powder	(optional)
	10 minutes +	1 tsp Madras curry powder	salt and pepper
	1¾ hours to marinate/cool	6 tbsp vegetable oil	
		600 g/1 lb 5 oz skinless,	TO SERVE
		boneless chicken breasts	freshly cooked Golden Rice
	55 minutes	500 ml/18 fl oz water	(see page 78)
		1 large garlic clove, finely chopped	Mango Chutney (see page 92)

Put the ginger, turmeric, cumin, garam masala, chilli powder, curry powder and 5 tablespoons of the oil into a bowl and mix together. Cut the chicken into bite-sized chunks, add to the bowl and stir until well coated. Cover with clingfilm and refrigerate for 1 hour.

Meanwhile, bring 300 ml/10 fl oz of the water to the boil in a small saucepan. Add the garlic, onions and half of the lemon juice, return to the boil and continue to boil for 5 minutes. Remove from the heat and leave to cool for 45 minutes. Transfer to a food processor and process for a few seconds.

Heat the remaining oil in a saucepan over a medium heat, add the chicken mixture and cook for 2 minutes. Stir in the onion mixture, tomato purée and the remaining water and lemon juice and bring to the boil. Continue to boil, stirring, for 15 minutes. Reduce the heat, stir in the food colouring and season. Cover and simmer for 30 minutes. Serve with freshly cooked rice and Mango Chutney.

chicken jalfrezi

		ingredients	
	very easy	1 red pepper, quartered and deseeded	1 tsp garam masala
		1 green pepper, quartered	4 skinless, boneless chicken breasts,
	serves 4	and deseeded	cut into bite-sized chunks
		3 tbsp ghee or butter	75 g/2¾ oz unsalted cashew
		1 tbsp chilli oil	nuts, halved
		1 large onion, finely chopped	100 ml/3½ fl oz natural yogurt
	25 minutes +	3 large garlic cloves, crushed	3 large tomatoes, peeled and chopped
	15 minutes	2.5-cm/1-inch piece fresh root	1 tbsp tomato purée
	to cool	ginger, grated	100 ml/3½ fl oz boiling water
		1 tsp chilli powder	
	45–50	1 tsp turmeric	TO SERVE
	minutes	1 tsp ground cumin	Naan Breads (see page 84)
		1 tsp ground coriander	Mango Chutney (see page 92)

Flatten the peppers, then place skin-side up on a grill pan. Cook under a preheated hot grill for 10 minutes, turning frequently, until blackened and blistered all over. Transfer to a polythene bag and leave until cool, then peel off the skins. Chop the flesh.

Heat the ghee and oil in a large saucepan over a medium heat. Add the onion, garlic and ginger and cook, stirring, for 4 minutes, or until softened and golden. Add the chilli powder, turmeric, cumin, coriander and garam masala and cook, stirring, for 1 minute. Add the chicken and cashew nuts and cook, stirring, for 5 minutes.

Remove from the heat and stir in the yogurt. Return to the heat and stir in the tomatoes, tomato purée, peppers and boiling water. Bring to the boil, then reduce the heat and simmer, stirring frequently, for 20–25 minutes, or until the sauce has thickened.

Serve with Naan Breads and Mango Chutney.

chicken korma

		ingredients	
	very easy	1 chicken, weighing 1.3 kg/3 lb	½ tsp ground cardamom
		225 g/8 oz ghee or butter	½ tsp ground cinnamon
	serves 4	3 onions, thinly sliced	½ tsp salt
		1 garlic clove, crushed	1 tbsp gram flour
		2.5-cm/1-inch piece fresh root	125 ml/4 fl oz milk
	20 minutes + 30 minutes to cool	ginger, grated	500 ml/18 fl oz double cream
		1 tsp mild chilli powder	
		1 tsp turmeric	fresh coriander leaves, to garnish
	1 hour 25 minutes	1 tsp ground coriander	freshly cooked rice, to serve

Put the chicken into a large saucepan, cover with water and bring to the boil. Reduce the heat, cover and simmer for 30 minutes. Remove from the heat, lift out the chicken and set aside to cool. Reserve 125 ml/4 fl oz of the cooking liquid. Remove and discard the skin and bones. Cut the flesh into bite-sized pieces.

Heat the ghee in a large saucepan over a medium heat. Add the onions and garlic and cook, stirring, for 3 minutes, or until softened. Add the ginger, chilli powder, turmeric, ground coriander, cardamom, cinnamon and salt and cook for a further 5 minutes. Add the chicken and the reserved cooking liquid. Cook for 2 minutes.

Blend the flour with a little of the milk and add to the pan, then stir in the remaining milk. Bring to the boil, stirring, then reduce the heat, cover and simmer for 25 minutes. Stir in the cream, cover and simmer for a further 15 minutes.

Garnish with coriander leaves and serve with freshly cooked rice.

thai red chicken curry

very easy	
serves 4	
30 minutes	
40 minutes	

ingredients

6 garlic cloves, chopped
2 fresh red chillies, chopped
2 tbsp chopped fresh lemon grass
1 tsp finely grated lime rind
1 tbsp chopped fresh kaffir lime leaves
1 tbsp Thai Red Curry Paste (see page 36)
1 tbsp coriander seeds,
   toasted and crushed
1 tbsp chilli oil
4 skinless, boneless chicken
   breasts, sliced
300 ml/10 fl oz coconut milk

300 ml/10 fl oz chicken stock
1 tbsp soy sauce
55 g/2 oz shelled unsalted peanuts,
   toasted and ground
3 spring onions, diagonally sliced
1 red pepper, deseeded and sliced
3 Thai aubergines, sliced
2 tbsp chopped fresh Thai basil or
   fresh coriander

fresh coriander, to garnish
freshly cooked jasmine rice, to serve

Put the garlic, chillies, lemon grass, lime rind, lime leaves, curry paste and coriander seeds into a food processor and process until the mixture is smooth.

Heat the oil in a wok or large frying pan over a high heat, add the chicken and garlic mixture and stir-fry for 5 minutes. Add the coconut milk, stock and soy sauce and bring to the boil. Reduce the heat and cook, stirring, for another 3 minutes. Stir in the ground peanuts and simmer for 20 minutes.

Add the spring onions, pepper and aubergines and simmer, stirring occasionally, for a further 10 minutes. Remove from the heat and stir in the basil and garnish with coriander. Serve immediately with freshly cooked jasmine rice.

green duck curry

		ingredients	
	very easy	10 fresh green chillies, deseeded and chopped	3 spring onions, chopped
			600 ml/1 pint coconut milk
	serves 4	2 tbsp chopped fresh galangal	950 g/2 lb 2 oz skinless duck meat, cut into slices or chunks
		1 tbsp chopped fresh lemon grass	
		1 tbsp chopped fresh root ginger	1 tbsp fish sauce
	25 minutes	4 garlic cloves, chopped	50 g/1¾ oz creamed coconut, grated
		6 black peppercorns, crushed	3 tbsp chopped fresh Thai basil or ordinary basil
		1 tsp ground cumin	
	1 hour 40 minutes	½ tsp salt	freshly cooked white rice, to serve
		1 tbsp chilli oil	

Preheat the oven to 180°C/350°F/Gas Mark 4.

Put 8 of the chillies into a food processor with the galangal, lemon grass, ginger, garlic, peppercorns, cumin, salt, oil and 2 of the spring onions. Process until smooth. Stir in the coconut milk.

Put the duck meat into a casserole dish and pour over the coconut milk mixture. Stir in the remaining chillies and spring onion, fish sauce and creamed coconut. Cover, transfer to the preheated oven and cook for 1 hour 40 minutes.

Remove from the oven and stir in the basil. Serve with freshly cooked rice.

lamb do piaza

very easy	
serves 4	
20 minutes	
45 minutes	

ingredients

4 onions, sliced into rings
3 garlic cloves, coarsely chopped
2.5-cm/1-inch piece fresh root
   ginger, grated
1 tsp ground coriander
1 tsp ground cumin
1 tsp chilli powder
½ tsp turmeric
1 tsp ground cinnamon
1 tsp garam masala

4 tbsp water
5 tbsp ghee or vegetable oil
600 g/1 lb 5 oz boneless lamb,
   cut into bite-sized chunks
6 tbsp natural yogurt
salt

fresh coriander leaves, to garnish
freshly cooked rice, to serve

Put half of the onion rings into a food processor with the garlic, ginger, ground coriander, cumin, chilli powder, turmeric, cinnamon and garam masala. Add the water and process to a paste.

Heat 4 tablespoons of the ghee in a saucepan over a medium heat. Add the remaining onions and cook, stirring, for 3 minutes. Remove from the heat. Lift out the onions with a slotted spoon and set aside. Heat the remaining ghee in the pan over a high heat, add the lamb and cook, stirring, for 5 minutes. Lift out the meat and drain on kitchen paper. Add the onion paste to the pan and cook over a medium heat, stirring, until the oil separates. Stir in the yogurt, season to taste, return the lamb to the pan and stir well.

Bring the mixture gently to the boil, reduce the heat, cover and simmer for 25 minutes. Stir in the reserved onion rings and cook for a further 5 minutes. Remove from the heat, pile on to freshly cooked rice and garnish with coriander leaves. Serve immediately.

rogan josh

		ingredients	
	very easy	125 ml/4 fl oz ghee or vegetable oil	4 cloves, ground
		500 g/1 lb 2 oz boneless lamb,	1 tsp coriander seeds, ground
	serves 4	cut into bite-sized chunks	1 tsp cumin seeds, ground
		4 garlic cloves, chopped	250 ml/9 fl oz soured cream
		3 fresh green chillies, chopped	½ tsp turmeric
	20 minutes +	2.5-cm/1-inch piece fresh root	½ tsp chilli powder
	15 minutes	ginger, grated	2 large tomatoes, chopped
	to cool	1 tsp poppy seeds	1 bay leaf
		1 cinnamon stick, ground	
	50–55	1 cardamom pod, ground	fresh coriander leaves, to garnish
	minutes		freshly cooked rice, to serve

Heat half of the ghee in a large saucepan over a high heat, add the lamb and cook, stirring, for 5 minutes. Lift out the meat with a slotted spoon and drain on kitchen paper. Add the garlic, chillies, ginger, poppy seeds and ground spices to the pan and cook over a medium heat, stirring, for 4 minutes. Remove from the heat, leave to cool for a few minutes, then transfer the spice mixture to a food processor. Stir in the soured cream, turmeric and chilli powder and process until smooth.

Heat the remaining ghee in the saucepan over a low heat, add the tomatoes and cook, stirring, for 3 minutes. Add the soured cream mixture and cook, stirring, until the oil separates. Remove from the heat and add the lamb. Add the bay leaf, return the pan to the heat and cover. Simmer gently for 35–40 minutes, or until most of the liquid has been absorbed. Remove from the heat and discard the bay leaf. Garnish with coriander leaves and serve with freshly cooked rice.

indonesian beef curry

		ingredients	
	very easy	4 tbsp chilli oil	½ tsp shrimp paste
		3 spring onions, sliced	300 ml/10 fl oz water
	serves 4	2 garlic cloves, chopped	300 ml/10 fl oz coconut milk
		2 fresh red chillies, chopped	4 tbsp coconut cream
		2.5-cm/1-inch piece fresh root	
	15–20 minutes	ginger, grated	2 tbsp chopped fresh coriander, to garnish
		950 g/2 lb 2 oz boneless lean beef, cut into bite-sized chunks	freshly cooked Asian Coconut Rice (see page 80), to serve
	1 hour 40 minutes	1 tsp ground cumin	
		1 tsp ground cinnamon	

Heat the oil in a wok or large frying pan over a medium heat. Add the spring onions, garlic, chillies and ginger and cook, stirring, for 3 minutes. Add the beef and stir-fry over a high heat for 5 minutes. Add the cumin, cinnamon, shrimp paste, water and coconut milk and bring to the boil, stirring. Reduce the heat, cover and simmer for 1 hour.

Stir in the coconut cream, cover and simmer for a further 30 minutes, until almost all the liquid has been absorbed.

Remove from the heat and pile on to freshly cooked rice. Sprinkle over the coriander and serve immediately.

spiced beef curry

		ingredients	
very easy			
serves 4	4 tbsp ghee or vegetable oil	1 tsp turmeric	
	450 g/1 lb boneless lean beef, cut into bite-sized chunks	1 tsp curry powder	
	2 large onions, sliced	1 tsp salt	
	2 large garlic cloves, chopped	½ tsp freshly ground black pepper	
20 minutes	2.5-cm/1-inch piece fresh root ginger, grated	4 tomatoes, chopped	
	2 fresh red chillies, chopped	1 red pepper, deseeded and chopped	
	100 g/3½ oz aubergine, chopped	1 tbsp tomato purée	
2 hours 10–15 minutes	2 tsp ground coriander	300 ml/10 fl oz water	
	1 tsp ground cumin	100 g/3½ oz carrots, thinly sliced	
		250 g/9 oz sweet potatoes, sliced	

Preheat the oven to 180°C/350°F/Gas Mark 4. Heat half of the ghee in a covered casserole dish over a high heat. Add the beef and cook, stirring, for 5 minutes. Lift out the meat with a slotted spoon and drain on kitchen paper. Heat the remaining ghee in the dish over a medium heat, add the onions, garlic, ginger, chillies and aubergine and cook, stirring, for 4 minutes. Add the coriander, cumin, turmeric, curry powder, salt and pepper and cook, stirring, for a further 3 minutes. Return the meat to the dish, then add the tomatoes, red pepper and tomato purée. Pour in the water and bring to the boil. Remove from the heat, cover and transfer to the oven. Cook for 1 hour 40 minutes.

About 15 minutes before the end of the cooking time, bring a saucepan of lightly salted water to the boil. Add the carrots and sweet potatoes and cook for 10 minutes. Remove from the heat and drain. Remove the dish from the oven and add the carrots and potatoes. Cover and cook for a further 10–15 minutes, then serve.

pork vindaloo

very easy	
serves 4	
20 minutes + 2–8 hours to marinate	
1 hour 10 minutes	

ingredients

1 tsp black peppercorns
1 tsp cumin seeds
1 tsp cardamom seeds
1 tsp mustard seeds
6 tbsp red wine vinegar
1 tsp ground coriander
½ tsp paprika
½ tsp sugar
900 g/2 lb lean pork,
  pricked with a fork
100 ml/3½ fl oz vegetable oil

1 onion, chopped
2 fresh red chillies, chopped
1 red pepper, deseeded and chopped
4 tomatoes, chopped
100 ml/3½ fl oz water
few drops of red food colouring
  (optional)

TO SERVE
Chapatis (see page 86)
Herb Raita (see page 90)

Dry-fry the peppercorns and cumin, cardamom and mustard seeds in a wok or frying pan over a low heat until lightly coloured. Transfer to a mortar and grind to a powder with a pestle. Add the vinegar, coriander, paprika and sugar and stir well.

Cut the pork into bite-sized chunks and arrange in a shallow non-metallic dish. Pour over the spiced vinegar mixture and mix well. Cover with clingfilm and refrigerate for at least 2 hours, or preferably overnight.

Heat the oil in a wok or large frying pan over a high heat, add the meat and marinade and cook, stirring, for 5 minutes. Add the onion, chillies, pepper, tomatoes and water and mix well. Stir in the red food colouring, if using. Bring to the boil, then reduce the heat, cover and simmer for 1 hour, or until the meat is tender and cooked through.

Serve with Chapatis and Herb Raita.

asian pork curry

		ingredients	
	very easy	2 tbsp chilli oil	1 tbsp fish sauce
		500 g/1 lb 2 oz lean pork,	2 tsp soy sauce
	serves 4	cut into bite-sized chunks	2 tsp sugar
		2 fresh red chillies, chopped	500 ml/18 fl oz coconut milk
		3 spring onions, sliced	1 large potato, cut into
	20 minutes	2 tbsp finely chopped fresh	bite-sized chunks
		lemon grass	75 g/2¾ oz shelled unsalted peanuts,
		1 tbsp grated fresh root ginger	toasted and crushed
	1¼ hours	1 tbsp curry paste	shredded fresh spring onion, to garnish
		2 tbsp yellow bean sauce	freshly cooked jasmine rice, to serve

Heat half of the oil in a wok or large frying pan over a high heat, add the pork and cook, stirring, for 5 minutes. Lift out the meat with a slotted spoon and drain on kitchen paper. Heat the remaining oil in the pan, add the chillies, spring onions, lemon grass and ginger and cook, stirring, for 4 minutes. Add the curry paste, yellow bean, fish and soy sauces and sugar and stir well. Add the meat and coconut milk and bring to the boil. Reduce the heat, cover and simmer for 40 minutes.

Add the potato, cover and cook for a further 20 minutes.

Stir in the crushed peanuts and cook for a further 5 minutes.

Garnish with shredded spring onion and serve with freshly cooked jasmine rice.

fish & seafood

Fish and seafood are healthy as well as delicious, and this exciting selection of recipes cannot fail to spice up any mealtime. If you are short of time, you can replace the green and red curry pastes in this section with shop-bought varieties, widely available from many supermarkets and specialist food outlets. These curry pastes can be used in many different dishes, however, so it is definitely worth making your own when you have the opportunity. They will add a unique blend of fragrant flavourings to all kinds of meat, fish and vegetable dishes.

green haddock curry

		ingredients	
	very easy	1 tbsp vegetable or chilli oil	2 tsp chopped fresh kaffir lime leaves
		400 ml/14 fl oz coconut milk	2 large garlic cloves, finely chopped
	serves 4	1 green pepper, deseeded and chopped	2.5-cm/1-inch piece fresh root
		1 tbsp chopped fresh lemon grass	ginger, grated
		800 g/1 lb 12 oz haddock fillets,	1 tbsp finely chopped fresh lemon grass
		rinsed and cut into bite-sized chunks	2 tsp ground coriander
	20–25	2½ tbsp fish sauce	½ tsp ground cumin
	minutes	2 tbsp chopped fresh coriander	½ tsp salt
			2 tbsp chilli oil
		GREEN CURRY PASTE	
	20 minutes	8 fresh green chillies, chopped	fresh coriander leaves, to garnish
		2 tbsp chopped spring onions	freshly cooked jasmine rice, to serve

To make the green curry paste, put all the ingredients into a food processor and process until smooth. Transfer to a bowl, cover with clingfilm and refrigerate until required.

Heat the oil in a large saucepan over a medium heat, add 3 tablespoons of the curry paste and cook, stirring, for 1 minute. Stir in 4 tablespoons of the coconut milk, then add the pepper and lemon grass. Cook, stirring, for 4 minutes. Add the haddock, fish sauce and remaining coconut milk. Bring to the boil, then reduce the heat and simmer for 10 minutes. Stir in the fresh coriander.

Remove from the heat and spoon on to freshly cooked jasmine rice. Garnish with coriander leaves and serve.

salmon curry

		ingredients	
very easy			
serves 4	1 tbsp vegetable or chilli oil	3 large garlic cloves, finely chopped	
	400 ml/14 fl oz coconut milk	2 tbsp chopped fresh galangal	
	1 red pepper, deseeded and chopped	1 tbsp chopped fresh lemon grass	
	1 tbsp chopped fresh lemon grass	2 tsp ground coriander	
20–25 minutes + 15–20 minutes to soak	800 g/1 lb 12 oz salmon fillets, rinsed and cut into bite-sized chunks	2 tsp shrimp paste	
	300 g/10½ oz frozen spinach	½ tsp salt	
		½ tsp cracked black peppercorns	
20 minutes	THAI RED CURRY PASTE		
	8 small, dried red chillies	2 tbsp chopped fresh Thai basil or ordinary basil, to garnish	
	3 tbsp chopped spring onions	freshly cooked rice, to serve	

To make the Thai red curry paste, deseed the chillies, put into
a bowl of hot water and leave to soak for 15–20 minutes.
Lift them out and coarsely chop. Put into a food processor with
the remaining ingredients and process until smooth. Transfer to
a bowl, cover with clingfilm and refrigerate until required.

Heat the oil in a large saucepan over a medium heat, add
3 tablespoons of the curry paste and cook, stirring, for 1 minute.
Stir in 4 tablespoons of the coconut milk, then add the pepper
and lemon grass. Cook, stirring, for 4 minutes. Add the salmon
and spinach, then stir in the remaining coconut milk. Bring to
the boil, then reduce the heat and simmer for 10 minutes.

Remove from the heat and spoon on to freshly cooked rice.
Garnish with basil and serve.

monkfish & coconut curry

		ingredients	
very easy	3 tbsp ghee or vegetable oil	500 ml/18 fl oz coconut milk
	2 onions, sliced	700 g/1 lb 9 oz monkfish fillets,
serves 4	3 garlic cloves, crushed	rinsed and cut into large chunks
	1 tbsp mustard seeds	
	1 fresh red chilli,	4 long, thin, fresh red chillies, cut into
15 minutes + 25–30 minutes to soak	deseeded and chopped	flowers (see below), to garnish
	½ tsp turmeric	freshly cooked noodles, to serve
	1 tsp ground fenugreek	
15–20 minutes		

To make the chilli flowers, use a sharp knife to make 6 cuts in each chilli. Start about 1 cm/½ inch from the stalk end and cut to the tip of each chilli. Put them in a bowl of iced water and leave for 25–30 minutes, or until they have opened out into flower shapes.

Heat the ghee in a large frying pan over a low heat, add the onions, garlic and mustard seeds and cook, stirring, for 4 minutes. Add the chilli, turmeric and fenugreek and cook for a further 2 minutes. Stir in 4 tablespoons of the coconut milk and mix well. Stir in the remaining coconut milk and bring to the boil. Reduce the heat, add the monkfish chunks and simmer, turning once, for 6–7 minutes.

Remove from the heat and spoon on to freshly cooked noodles. Garnish with the chilli flowers and serve immediately.

halibut curry

		ingredients	
very easy		4 garlic cloves, chopped	400 ml/14 fl oz coconut milk
		1 fresh red chilli,	1 tbsp finely grated lime rind
serves 4		deseeded and chopped	salt and pepper
		1 tbsp chopped fresh galangal	650 g/1 lb 7 oz halibut fillets,
		150 ml/5 fl oz water	rinsed and cut into large chunks
15 minutes		4 tbsp vegetable oil	
		4 spring onions, sliced	thin strips of lime and lemon zest,
		2 tsp ground cumin	to garnish
		½ tsp turmeric	freshly cooked Asian Coconut Rice
35 minutes		½ tsp paprika	(see page 80), to serve

Put the garlic, chilli, galangal and water into a food processor and process until smooth.

Heat the oil in a large saucepan over a medium heat, add the spring onions and cook, stirring, for 5 minutes. Add the cumin, turmeric, paprika and chilli mixture and cook, stirring, for 4 minutes. Stir in the coconut milk and lime rind and season to taste with salt and pepper. Bring to the boil, then continue to boil for 15 minutes.

Reduce the heat, add the halibut and turn in the sauce to coat evenly. Simmer for 5–6 minutes, turning once, until tender.

Remove from the heat and spoon on to freshly cooked Asian Coconut Rice. Garnish with strips of lemon and lime zest and serve immediately.

curried fish stew

		ingredients	
very easy		350 g/12 oz halibut fillets, rinsed and cut into large chunks	1 tbsp grated fresh galangal
serves 4		350 g/12 oz cod fillets, rinsed and cut into large chunks	2 tsp curry powder
		½ tsp salt	400 ml/14 fl oz coconut milk
15 minutes + 45 minutes to marinate		2 limes	salt and pepper
		3 tbsp vegetable oil	thin strips of lemon zest, to garnish
		4 spring onions, chopped	TO SERVE
		3 garlic cloves, chopped	lime wedges
25 minutes		3 fresh green chillies, deseeded and chopped	freshly cooked rice

Arrange the fish in a shallow non-metallic dish and sprinkle over the salt. Squeeze over the limes until all their juice has been extracted, then cover the dish with clingfilm and refrigerate for 45 minutes.

Heat the oil in a large frying pan over a low heat, add the spring onions and garlic and cook, stirring, for 3 minutes. Add the chillies and galangal and cook, stirring, for a further 2 minutes. Stir in the curry powder and coconut milk and season to taste with salt and pepper. Bring gently to a simmer, then continue to simmer for 10 minutes. Add the fish and turn in the sauce to coat. Cook for about 5 minutes, turning once, or until cooked through. Adjust the seasoning.

Serve with lime wedges and freshly cooked rice.

seafood laksa

		ingredients	
very easy	200 g/7 oz live mussels, scrubbed and debearded	2 tsp ground cumin
	250 g/9 oz rice noodles	450 ml/16 fl oz coconut milk
serves 4	2 tbsp chilli oil	450 ml/16 fl oz fish stock or water
	3 garlic cloves, chopped	1 tbsp rice wine or sherry
	3 spring onions, diagonally sliced	1 tbsp soy sauce
25 minutes + 10 minutes to soak	3 fresh green chillies, deseeded and chopped	150 g/5½ oz cod fillets, rinsed and cut into chunks
	1 tbsp chopped fresh lemon grass	150 g/5½ oz raw prawns, peeled and deveined
20 minutes	1 tbsp Thai Red Curry Paste (see page 36)	4 whole tiger prawns, cooked, to garnish

Discard any mussels with broken shells or any that refuse to close when tapped. Put the remaining mussels into a saucepan with a little water over a high heat, cover and bring to the boil. Cook for 4 minutes, shaking the pan occasionally. Remove the mussels from the heat, drain and reserve, discarding any that remain closed.

Cook the noodles in a large saucepan of lightly salted boiling water for 2 minutes. Drain well, then divide between 4 soup bowls.

Heat the oil in a saucepan over a medium heat, add the garlic and spring onions and cook, stirring, for 4 minutes. Add the chillies, lemon grass, curry paste and cumin and cook, stirring, for a further 3 minutes. Stir in the coconut milk, fish stock, rice wine and soy sauce, bring to the boil, then reduce the heat, add the cod and mussels and cook for 3 minutes. Add the prawns and cook for 2 minutes. Pour over the noodles in the soup bowls. Garnish with tiger prawns and serve.

prawn masala

		ingredients	
very easy	2 fresh red chillies, deseeded and chopped	300 ml/10 fl oz natural yogurt
	2 garlic cloves, chopped	2 tbsp chopped fresh coriander
serves 4	½ onion, chopped	500 g/1 lb 2 oz raw tiger prawns, peeled and tails left intact
	2.5-cm/1-inch piece fresh root ginger, chopped	sprigs of fresh coriander, to garnish
20 minutes + 1–1½ hours to marinate	1 tsp turmeric	TO SERVE
	1 tsp ground cumin	lime wedges
	1 tsp garam masala	Naan Breads (see page 84) or freshly cooked rice
4 minutes	½ tsp sugar	
	½ tsp freshly ground black pepper	

Put the chillies into a food processor with the garlic, onion, ginger, turmeric, cumin, garam masala, sugar, pepper and yogurt. Process until smooth, then transfer to a large, shallow dish. Stir in the coriander. Thread the prawns on to skewers, leaving a small space at either end. Transfer them to the dish and turn in the mixture until thoroughly coated. Cover with clingfilm and refrigerate for 1–1½ hours.

Remove from the refrigerator and arrange the skewers on a grill rack lined with foil. Cook under a preheated medium grill, turning and basting with the marinade, for 4 minutes, until sizzling and cooked through.

Garnish with coriander sprigs and serve with lime wedges and Naan Breads.

prawn & kidney bean curry

	ingredients	
very easy	2 tbsp ghee or chilli oil	200 g/7 oz canned chickpeas,
	1 onion, chopped	rinsed and drained
	2 garlic cloves, chopped	salt and pepper
serves 4	2.5-cm/1-inch piece fresh	500 g/1 lb 2 oz raw prawns,
	galangal, chopped	peeled and deveined
	1 tsp curry powder	5 tbsp natural yogurt
	1 tsp ground coriander	1 tbsp finely grated lemon rind
15 minutes	1 tsp ground cumin	3 tbsp chopped fresh parsley
	1 tsp turmeric	
	3 tomatoes, peeled and chopped	TO SERVE
	150 ml/5 fl oz fish stock	freshly cooked rice
35 minutes	200 g/7 oz canned red kidney beans,	lemon wedges
	rinsed and drained	

Heat the ghee in a large saucepan over a low heat. Add the onion, garlic and galangal and cook, stirring, for 4 minutes. Add the curry powder, coriander, cumin and turmeric and cook, stirring, for a further 3 minutes. Add the tomatoes, stock, beans and chickpeas and season to taste with salt and pepper. Bring gently to the boil, then reduce the heat and simmer for 20 minutes.

Add the prawns and cook, stirring gently, for 2–3 minutes. Stir in the yogurt, lemon rind and parsley and heat through.

Remove from the heat, spoon over freshly cooked rice and serve with lemon wedges.

red mussel curry

very easy	
serves 4	
20 minutes + 10 minutes to soak	
20 minutes	

ingredients

1 kg/2 lb 4 oz live mussels
1 tbsp chilli oil
1½ tbsp Thai Red Curry Paste
   (see page 36)
1 fresh red chilli,
   deseeded and chopped
1 tbsp chopped fresh lemon grass
1 tsp sugar

2 tbsp fish sauce
600 ml/1 pint coconut milk
1 tbsp finely grated lime rind
3 tbsp chopped fresh coriander

chopped fresh parsley, to garnish
freshly cooked noodles, to serve

To prepare the mussels, soak them in lightly salted water for 10 minutes. Scrub under cold running water and pull off any beards. Discard any mussels with broken shells or any that refuse to close when tapped. Put the remaining mussels into a saucepan with a little water over a high heat, cover and bring to the boil. Cook for 4 minutes, shaking the pan occasionally. Remove the mussels from the heat, drain and reserve, discarding any that remain closed.

Heat the oil in a large saucepan over a medium heat, add the curry paste, chilli and lemon grass and cook, stirring, for 4 minutes. Add the sugar and fish sauce and cook, stirring, for a further 2 minutes. Stir in 4 tablespoons of the coconut milk, then stir in the remaining coconut milk. Bring to the boil, then reduce the heat, add the reserved mussels and cook for 3 minutes. Stir in the lime rind and coriander and cook for a further 1–2 minutes. Remove from the heat and spoon over freshly cooked noodles. Garnish with parsley and serve immediately.

vegetables

This chapter contains an inspiring array of meatless dishes from around the world that are sure to delight meat-eaters as well as vegetarians. Who will be able to resist the fruity Caribbean Curry or the tangy Thai Green Curry? There are also more familiar favourites on offer, such as the mild and creamy Vegetable Korma and the comforting Spicy Dhal. The Vegetable Samosas and Onion Bhajis make ideal lunchbox and picnic fare, and you can also serve them at home as a delicious snack, lunch or light supper. Either way, your household will be clamouring for more.

fragrant vegetable curry

		ingredients	
	very easy	200 g/7 oz potatoes, cut into chunks 200 g/7 oz sweet potatoes, cut into chunks	1 tsp ground coriander 1 tsp ground cumin 1 tsp turmeric
	serves 4	200 g/7 oz carrots, cut into chunks 1 parsnip, chopped 3 tbsp ghee or vegetable oil	350 ml/12 fl oz vegetable stock 200 ml/7 fl oz coconut cream salt and pepper
	15 minutes	1 onion, chopped 3 garlic cloves, chopped 2.5-cm/1-inch piece fresh root ginger, grated 1 aubergine, cut into chunks	fresh coriander leaves, to garnish TO SERVE freshly cooked Asian Coconut Rice (see page 80)
	1¼ hours	1 fresh red chilli, chopped 1 tsp tamarind paste	Spicy Chickpeas (see page 82)

Preheat the oven to 180°C/350°F/Gas Mark 4.

Bring a large saucepan of water to the boil, add the potatoes and sweet potatoes and cook for 5 minutes. Add the carrots and parsnip and cook for a further 5 minutes. Drain, refresh under cold running water, then drain again.

Heat the ghee in a flameproof casserole dish over a medium heat, add the onion and garlic and cook, stirring, for 3 minutes. Add the ginger, aubergine and chilli and cook, stirring, for a further 3 minutes. Stir in the tamarind paste, ground coriander, cumin, turmeric, stock and coconut cream, then add the cooked vegetables and season to taste with salt and pepper. Bring to the boil, stirring, then reduce the heat and simmer for 2 minutes.

Cover and transfer to the preheated oven. Cook for 50 minutes. Remove from the oven, spoon over Asian Coconut Rice, garnish and serve with Spicy Chickpeas.

spicy dhal

		ingredients	

very easy		200 g/7 oz red lentils
		1 cardamom pod
		1 tsp mustard seeds
		1 tsp cumin seeds
		100 ml/3½ fl oz ghee or vegetable oil
		2 onions, chopped
		2 garlic cloves, chopped
		400 g/14 oz canned chopped tomatoes
		  in their juice
		200 g/7 oz sweet potato, chopped
		4 tbsp vegetable stock
			salt and pepper
			400 g/14 oz canned chickpeas,
			  rinsed and drained
			1 tsp turmeric
			1 tsp ground coriander
			1 tsp chilli powder
			1 tsp garam masala
			100 g/3½ oz frozen spinach
			
			TO SERVE
			Chapatis (see page 86)
			Lime Pickle (see page 94)

serves 4			
20 minutes + 2–8 hours to soak			
1 hour 15 minutes			

Rinse the lentils under running water, removing any that discolour. Bring a large saucepan of water to the boil and add the lentils. Cook for 20–25 minutes, or until tender, then drain and set aside.

Split the cardamom pod and crush the seeds with the mustard and cumin seeds. Heat the ghee in a saucepan over a low heat, add the seeds and cook, stirring, for a few seconds. Add the onions and garlic and cook, stirring, for 4 minutes. Add the tomatoes, sweet potato and stock and season to taste. Bring to the boil, then reduce the heat and cook, stirring occasionally, for 30 minutes.

Remove from the heat. Add the lentils, then lightly mash the mixture. Return to the heat and cook for a further 10 minutes. Add the chickpeas, turmeric, coriander, chilli powder and garam masala. Stir well, then stir in the spinach. Cook for a further 4–5 minutes. Serve with Chapatis and Lime Pickle.

vegetable korma

		ingredients	
	very easy	4 tbsp ghee or vegetable oil	½ tsp salt
		2 onions, chopped	1 tsp turmeric
	serves 4	2 garlic cloves, chopped	1 tsp ground cumin
		1 fresh red chilli, chopped	1 tsp ground coriander
		1 tbsp grated fresh root ginger	1 tsp garam masala
	20 minutes	2 tomatoes, peeled and chopped	200 ml/7 fl oz vegetable stock or water
		1 orange pepper, deseeded and cut into small pieces	150 ml/5 fl oz natural yogurt
			150 ml/5 fl oz single cream
	45 minutes	1 large potato, cut into chunks	25 g/1 oz fresh coriander, chopped
		200 g/7 oz cauliflower florets	freshly cooked rice, to serve

Heat the ghee in a large saucepan over a medium heat, add the onions and garlic and cook, stirring, for 3 minutes. Add the chilli and ginger and cook for a further 4 minutes. Add the tomatoes, pepper, potato, cauliflower, salt and spices and cook, stirring, for a further 3 minutes. Stir in the stock and bring to the boil. Reduce the heat and simmer for 25 minutes.

Stir in the yogurt and cream and cook, stirring, for a further 5 minutes. Add the fresh coriander and heat through.

Serve with freshly cooked rice.

mixed vegetable & nut curry

		ingredients	
very easy		200 g/7 oz broccoli florets	4 tomatoes, peeled and chopped
		150 g/5½ oz sugar snap peas	1 tsp chilli powder
serves 4		5 tbsp ghee or vegetable oil	1 tsp ground coriander
		2 garlic cloves, chopped	1 tbsp rice wine or sherry
		1 onion, finely sliced	1 tbsp soy sauce
15 minutes		1 fresh red chilli,	salt and pepper
		deseeded and chopped	3 tbsp grated coconut
		1 tbsp chopped fresh root ginger	90 g/3¼ oz unsalted cashew
		½ tbsp finely chopped lemon grass	nuts, halved
10–15 minutes		200 g/7 oz mycoprotein,	
		cut into chunks	fresh coconut shavings, to garnish
			freshly cooked rice noodles, to serve

Bring a large saucepan of water to the boil, add the broccoli and sugar snap peas and cook for 2 minutes. Drain, refresh under cold running water, then drain again.

Heat the ghee in a large wok or frying pan over a medium heat, add the garlic and onion and cook, stirring, for 3 minutes. Add the broccoli and sugar snap peas and cook for 2 minutes. Add the chilli, ginger, lemon grass, mycoprotein, tomatoes, chilli powder, coriander, rice wine and soy sauce and cook, stirring, for a further 2 minutes. Season to taste with salt and pepper. Add the grated coconut and cashew nuts and cook, stirring, for a further minute.

Remove from the heat and spoon on to freshly cooked rice noodles. Garnish with coconut shavings and serve.

asian egg curry

very easy	
serves 4	
15 minutes	
30 minutes	

ingredients

200 g/7 oz cauliflower florets	1 tsp ground coriander
4 tbsp chilli or vegetable oil	500 ml/18 fl oz coconut milk
2 garlic cloves, chopped	salt and pepper
3 spring onions, finely sliced	6 fresh kaffir lime leaves,
2 fresh red chillies,	finely shredded
deseeded and chopped	2 tbsp chopped fresh coriander
1 tbsp chopped fresh lemon grass	8 eggs, hard-boiled and cut into
4 tomatoes, chopped	quarters or thick slices
2 tsp turmeric	
1 tsp paprika	fresh coriander leaves, to garnish
	freshly cooked noodles, to serve

Bring a large saucepan of water to the boil, add the cauliflower and cook for 2 minutes. Drain, refresh under cold running water, then drain again.

Heat the oil in a large saucepan over a medium heat, add the garlic and spring onions and cook, stirring, for 3 minutes. Add the chillies and lemon grass and cook, stirring, for 2 minutes. Add the tomatoes, turmeric, paprika and ground coriander and cook, stirring, for a further 2 minutes. Stir in 4 tablespoons of the coconut milk, then stir in the remaining coconut milk. Season to taste with salt and pepper. Bring gently to the boil, then reduce the heat and simmer for 12 minutes. Add the cauliflower and cook for a further 3 minutes. Stir in the lime leaves and fresh coriander and heat through for 1 minute.

Remove from the heat, add the egg pieces and mix together gently. Spoon on to freshly cooked noodles, garnish and serve.

thai green curry

		ingredients	
	very easy	150 g/5½ oz broccoli florets	1 yellow pepper, deseeded and sliced
		150 g/5½ oz mangetout	1 tbsp soy sauce
	serves 4	2 tbsp chilli oil	100 g/3½ oz beansprouts
		2 tbsp Green Curry Paste (see page 34)	1 tbsp chopped fresh coriander
		350 ml/12 fl oz coconut milk	salt and pepper
	15 minutes	200 g/7 oz firm marinated tofu, cut into cubes	fresh sprigs of coriander, to garnish
		1 green pepper, deseeded and sliced	freshly cooked noodles, to serve
	20 minutes		

Bring a large saucepan of water to the boil, add the broccoli and mangetout and cook for 2 minutes. Drain, refresh under cold running water, then drain again.

Heat the oil in a large saucepan over a medium heat, add the curry paste and cook, stirring, for 1 minute. Stir in 4 tablespoons of the coconut milk, then add the tofu, broccoli, mangetout, peppers and soy sauce. Cook for 5 minutes, then stir in the remaining coconut milk and bring to the boil. Reduce the heat, add the beansprouts and cook for a further 5 minutes. Stir in the chopped coriander, season to taste with salt and pepper and heat through.

Remove from the heat and spoon on to freshly cooked noodles. Garnish with coriander leaves and serve.

caribbean curry

very easy	
serves 4	
15–20 minutes	
15 minutes	

ingredients

4 tbsp butter
2 large, slightly underripe bananas, thickly sliced
1 onion, thickly sliced
4 cabbage leaves (tough stalks removed), finely shredded
1 tbsp finely grated orange rind
1 tsp ground coriander
1 tsp cumin
1 tsp turmeric
1 tsp chilli powder
400 g/14 oz canned mixed beans, rinsed and drained

2 tbsp grated coconut
60 g/2¼ oz stoned dates, chopped
1 tbsp rum or orange juice
2 tbsp chopped fresh coriander
150 ml/5 fl oz single cream
50 g/1¾ oz shelled unsalted peanuts, halved and toasted

TO GARNISH
fresh coriander leaves
coconut shavings

freshly cooked rice, to serve

Heat the butter in a large frying pan over a low heat, add the bananas and cook for 2 minutes, or until lightly golden. Lift out with a slotted spoon and keep warm.

Add the onion to the pan and cook over a medium heat, stirring, for 4 minutes. Add the cabbage and orange rind, then the ground coriander, cumin, turmeric and chilli powder. Cook, stirring, for 2 minutes. Add the beans, grated coconut, dates and rum and cook, stirring, for a further 5 minutes. Stir in the chopped coriander, cream and peanuts and gently heat through for a further 1–2 minutes. Add the bananas and mix together gently.

Remove from the heat and spoon on to freshly cooked rice. Sprinkle over some coriander leaves and coconut shavings and serve.

baigan bharta

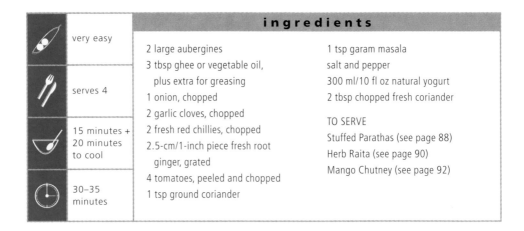

		ingredients	
very easy		2 large aubergines 3 tbsp ghee or vegetable oil, plus extra for greasing 1 onion, chopped 2 garlic cloves, chopped	1 tsp garam masala salt and pepper 300 ml/10 fl oz natural yogurt 2 tbsp chopped fresh coriander
serves 4		2 fresh red chillies, chopped 2.5-cm/1-inch piece fresh root ginger, grated	TO SERVE Stuffed Parathas (see page 88) Herb Raita (see page 90)
15 minutes + 20 minutes to cool		4 tomatoes, peeled and chopped 1 tsp ground coriander	Mango Chutney (see page 92)
30–35 minutes			

Preheat the oven to 240°C/475°F/Gas Mark 9. Lightly grease a baking sheet.

Cut the aubergines in half lengthways and place them, cut side down, on the baking sheet. Transfer to the oven and bake for 15–20 minutes, or until softened. Remove from the oven and leave to cool. Scoop out and chop the flesh, discarding the shells.

Heat the ghee in a large frying pan or saucepan over a medium heat, add the onion and garlic and cook, stirring, for 3 minutes. Add the chillies, ginger, tomatoes, ground coriander and garam masala and season to taste. Cook for 5 minutes. Add the reserved aubergine flesh and cook, stirring, for a further 5 minutes. Stir in the yogurt and fresh coriander and heat through gently for 1–2 minutes. Remove from the heat and serve immediately with Stuffed Parathas, Herb Raita and Mango Chutney.

vegetable samosas

easy	
serves 4	
20–25 minutes + 15 minutes to cool	
30 minutes	

ingredients

FILLING
1 medium carrot, diced
200 g/7 oz sweet potato, diced
85 g/3 oz frozen peas
2 tbsp ghee or vegetable oil
1 onion, chopped
1 garlic clove, chopped
2.5-cm/1-inch piece fresh root
  ginger, grated
1 tsp turmeric
1 tsp ground cumin
½ tsp chilli powder
½ tsp garam masala

1 tsp lime juice
salt and pepper
vegetable oil, for frying

PASTRY
150 g/5½ oz plain flour,
  plus extra for dusting
3 tbsp butter, diced
4 tbsp warm milk

TO SERVE
lime wedges
Mango Chutney (see page 92)

Bring a saucepan of water to the boil, add the carrot and cook for 4 minutes. Add the sweet potato and cook for 4 minutes, then add the peas and cook for 3 minutes. Drain. Heat the ghee in a saucepan over a medium heat, add the onion, garlic, ginger, spices and lime juice and cook, stirring, for 3 minutes. Add the vegetables and season. Cook, stirring, for 2 minutes. Remove from the heat, leave to cool a little, then mash.

Put the flour into a bowl and rub in the butter. Add the milk and mix to form a dough. Knead briefly and divide into 4. On a lightly floured work surface, roll into balls, then roll out into circles 17 cm/ 6½ inches in diameter. Halve each circle, divide the filling between them and brush the edges with water, then fold over into triangles and seal the edges. Heat 2.5 cm/1 inch of oil in a frying pan to 190°C/375°F, or until a cube of bread browns in 30 seconds. Cook the samosas in batches for 3–4 minutes, or until golden. Drain on kitchen paper and serve with lime wedges and Mango Chutney.

onion bhajis

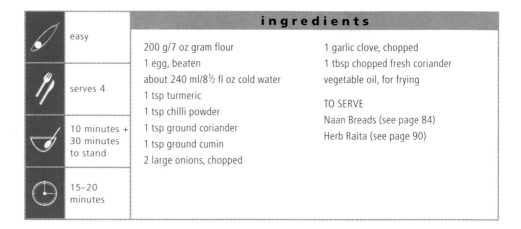

easy	
serves 4	
10 minutes + 30 minutes to stand	
15–20 minutes	

ingredients

200 g/7 oz gram flour
1 egg, beaten
about 240 ml/8½ fl oz cold water
1 tsp turmeric
1 tsp chilli powder
1 tsp ground coriander
1 tsp ground cumin
2 large onions, chopped

1 garlic clove, chopped
1 tbsp chopped fresh coriander
vegetable oil, for frying

TO SERVE
Naan Breads (see page 84)
Herb Raita (see page 90)

Put the flour into a large bowl and mix in the egg. Gradually mix in enough of the water to make a smooth, thick batter. Stir in the turmeric, chilli powder, ground coriander and cumin. Cover with clingfilm and leave to stand for 20 minutes.

Remove the clingfilm and stir in the onions, garlic and fresh coriander. Mix well, replace the clingfilm and leave to stand for a further 10 minutes.

Heat 2.5 cm/1 inch of oil in a large frying pan to 190°C/375°F, or until a cube of bread browns in 30 seconds. Drop a tablespoonful of the batter into the hot oil and cook, turning, until golden. Lift out with a slotted spoon and drain on kitchen paper. Cook the remaining bhajis in batches and drain on kitchen paper.

Serve with Naan Breads and Herb Raita.

sag aloo

very easy	
serves 4	
15 minutes	
40 minutes	

ingredients

550 g/1 lb 4 oz frozen spinach	1 tsp turmeric
6 tbsp ghee or vegetable oil	½ tsp paprika
1 onion, sliced	250 g/9 oz potatoes, coarsely chopped
2 garlic cloves, chopped	250 g/9 oz sweet potatoes,
2.5-cm/1-inch piece fresh root ginger,	coarsely chopped
finely sliced	4 tbsp water
1 fresh red chilli, chopped	salt and pepper

Bring a saucepan of water to the boil, add the spinach and return to the boil. Reduce the heat to medium and cook for 3 minutes. Drain and refresh under cold running water. Squeeze out any excess water from the spinach, then chop and set aside.

Heat the ghee in a large saucepan over a medium heat, add the onion and garlic and cook, stirring, for 2 minutes. Add the spinach and the remaining ingredients and bring to a simmer, then reduce the heat and cover. Continue to simmer for 30 minutes, or until the potatoes are tender, stirring occasionally and adding a little more water when necessary.

Remove from the heat and serve immediately.

side dishes

Every delicious curried dish in this book
deserves to have an equally well-crafted
accompaniment. In this chapter you will
find a range of enticing recipes that fit the
bill perfectly, starting with two exciting rice
dishes specially designed to complement
the main courses featured. The Naan Breads
and Chapatis are just the job for mopping
up the wonderfully spicy sauces, and the
Herb Raita, Mango Chutney and Lime Pickle
offer, in their individual ways, an interesting
contrast to the other aromatic flavours in
each meal.

golden rice

very easy	
serves 4	
10 minutes	
35–40 minutes	

ingredients

1 tsp saffron threads	½ tsp paprika
2 tbsp hot water	3 bay leaves
2 tbsp ghee or vegetable oil	400 g/14 oz long-grain rice,
3 onions, chopped	rinsed and drained
3 tbsp butter	about 850 ml/1½ pints vegetable
1 tsp ground cumin	stock or water
1 tsp cinnamon	100 g/3½ oz cashew nut
1 tsp salt	halves, toasted
½ tsp freshly ground black pepper	

Put the saffron threads and hot water into a small dish and set aside to soak.

Meanwhile, heat the ghee in a large saucepan over a low heat, add the onions and cook, stirring, for 5 minutes. Add the butter, cumin, cinnamon, salt, pepper, paprika and bay leaves and cook, stirring, for 2 minutes. Add the rice and cook, stirring, for 3 minutes. Add the saffron and pour in the stock. Bring to the boil, then reduce the heat, cover and simmer for 20–25 minutes, or until all the liquid has been absorbed. If the rice grains have not cooked through, add a little more stock and cook until tender and all the liquid has been absorbed.

Remove from the heat and discard the bay leaves. Adjust the seasoning. Add the cashew nuts and stir. Serve hot.

asian coconut rice

		ingredients	
	very easy	2 tbsp vegetable oil	1 tbsp freshly chopped lemon grass
		1 onion, chopped	500 ml/18 fl oz coconut milk
	serves 4	400 g/14 oz long-grain rice,	400 ml/14 fl oz water
		rinsed and drained	6 tbsp flaked coconut, toasted
	8–10 minutes		
	30–35 minutes		

Heat the oil in a large saucepan over a low heat, add the onion and cook, stirring, for 3 minutes. Add the rice and lemon grass and cook, stirring, for a further 2 minutes. Stir in the coconut milk and water and bring to the boil. Reduce the heat, cover and simmer for 20–25 minutes, or until all the liquid has been absorbed. If the rice grains have not cooked through, add a little more water and cook until tender and all the liquid has been absorbed.

Remove from the heat and add half of the flaked coconut. Stir gently. Scatter over the remaining coconut flakes and serve.

spicy chickpeas

		ingredients	
	very easy	2 tbsp ghee or vegetable oil	1 tsp garam masala
		1 onion, sliced	3 tomatoes, chopped
	serves 4	2 garlic cloves, chopped	1 tbsp tamarind paste
		2.5-cm/1-inch piece fresh root ginger, grated	300 g/10½ oz frozen chopped spinach
			400 g/14 oz canned chickpeas, drained
	10 minutes	2 fresh green chillies, chopped	½ tsp salt
		1 tsp ground cumin	½ tsp paprika
		1 tsp ground coriander	
	20 minutes		

Heat the ghee in a large saucepan over a low heat, add the onion and garlic and cook, stirring, for 5 minutes. Add the ginger, chillies, cumin, coriander and garam masala. Cook, stirring, for a further 2 minutes.

Add the tomatoes, then stir in the tamarind and spinach. Increase the heat to medium and cook, stirring, for 5 minutes, or until the spinach has thawed and any liquid has been absorbed.

Stir in the chickpeas, salt and paprika and cook, stirring, for a further 3 minutes.

Remove from the heat and serve.

naan breads

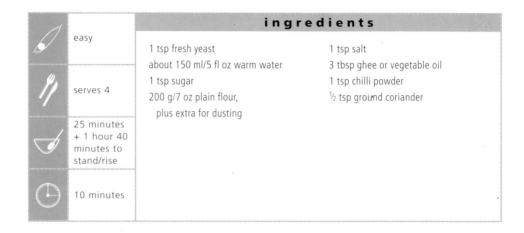

		ingredients	
easy	1 tsp fresh yeast	1 tsp salt
	about 150 ml/5 fl oz warm water	3 tbsp ghee or vegetable oil
serves 4	1 tsp sugar	1 tsp chilli powder
	200 g/7 oz plain flour,	½ tsp ground coriander
25 minutes + 1 hour 40 minutes to stand/rise	plus extra for dusting	
10 minutes		

Mix together the yeast, water and sugar in a bowl and set aside for 10 minutes.

Sift the flour and salt into a separate bowl. Make a well in the centre, add 1 tablespoon of the ghee and pour in the yeast mixture. Gradually mix in the flour from the sides to form a smooth dough and shape into a ball. Turn out on to a lightly floured work surface and knead for 5 minutes. Return to the bowl, cover and leave in a warm place for 1½ hours, or until doubled in size.

Knead the dough again for 3 minutes. Divide into 8 pieces and use your hands to shape them into balls. Flatten them into ovals 0.5 cm/¼ inch thick. Mix together the chilli powder and coriander, then turn the naan breads in the spice mixture until evenly coated.

Line a grill rack with foil and brush with ghee. Arrange the naans on top and brush with ghee. Cook under a preheated hot grill for 10 minutes, turning and brushing with more ghee, and serve.

chapatis

		ingredients	
easy		225 g/8 oz chapati flour or wholemeal flour, plus extra for dusting 1 tsp salt 1 tbsp ghee or vegetable oil	125 ml/4 fl oz water 1 tsp chilli powder 1 tsp ground coriander
serves 4			
20 minutes + 30 minutes to rest			
10 minutes			

Sift the flour and salt into a bowl. Make a well in the centre, add the ghee, then gradually mix in the water to form a smooth dough. Use your hands to shape the dough into a ball. Turn out on to a lightly floured work surface and knead for 8–10 minutes. Return to the bowl, cover with clingfilm and leave to rest for 30 minutes.

Divide the dough into 12 pieces and use your hands to shape them into balls. Roll out into rounds 15 cm/6 inches thick on a lightly floured work surface. Mix together the chilli powder and coriander, then turn the chapatis in the spice mixture until evenly coated.

Heat a large frying pan or ridged grill pan over a medium-high heat. When very hot, add a chapati and cook for 30 seconds, or until it starts to bubble. Turn over and gently press the chapati down. Cook for a few seconds, then lift out and keep warm in foil while you cook the remainder. When they are all cooked, serve immediately, or keep in the foil until ready to serve.

stuffed parathas

		ingredients	
	easy	**DOUGH**	**FILLING**
		100 g/3½ oz plain white flour	150 g/5½ oz sweet potatoes,
	serves 4	125 g/4½ oz wholemeal flour,	boiled and mashed
		plus extra for dusting	3 fresh green chillies, chopped
		1 tsp salt	½ onion, chopped and sautéed in
	35 minutes +	1 tbsp ghee or vegetable oil,	1 tbsp ghee or vegetable oil
	30 minutes	plus extra for brushing	1 tbsp chopped fresh coriander
	to rest	125 ml/4 fl oz warm water	1 tbsp chopped fresh parsley
			salt and pepper
	10 minutes		

Sift the flours and salt into a large bowl. Make a well in the centre, add the ghee, then gradually mix in the water to form a smooth dough. Use your hands to shape the dough into a ball. Turn out on to a lightly floured work surface and knead for 8–10 minutes. Leave to rest for 30 minutes.

To make the filling, mix all the ingredients together in a bowl and season to taste with salt and pepper.

Divide the dough into 4 pieces, shape into balls, then roll out gently into rounds on a lightly floured work surface. Put a spoonful of filling in the centre of each round. Gather up the sides and work into balls, then roll out gently into rounds and brush with ghee.

Heat a frying pan over a medium-high heat. When very hot, add a paratha and cook for 45 seconds, then turn over and cook on the other side for 30 seconds, or until lightly browned. Lift out and keep warm in foil while you cook the remainder. Serve immediately.

herb raita

		ingredients	
	extremely easy	350 ml/12 fl oz thick natural yogurt 60 g/2¼ oz fresh coriander, chopped 60 g/2¼ oz fresh parsley, chopped 25 g/1 oz fresh mint, chopped	1 fresh green chilli, deseeded and chopped ½ tsp salt
	serves 4		
	10 minutes		
	—		

To make the raita, put all the ingredients into a food processor and process until smooth. Transfer the raita to a serving bowl or individual serving dishes, cover with clingfilm and refrigerate until ready to serve.

mango chutney

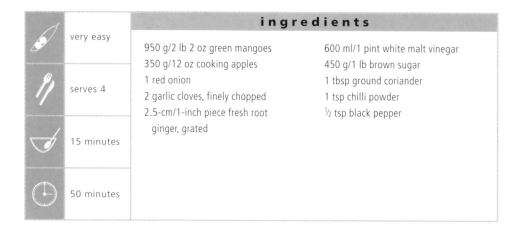

		ingredients	
very easy	950 g/2 lb 2 oz green mangoes	600 ml/1 pint white malt vinegar
	350 g/12 oz cooking apples	450 g/1 lb brown sugar
	1 red onion	1 tbsp ground coriander
serves 4	2 garlic cloves, finely chopped	1 tsp chilli powder
	2.5-cm/1-inch piece fresh root	½ tsp black pepper
	ginger, grated	
15 minutes		
50 minutes		

Peel and stone the mangoes and chop the flesh into bite-sized pieces. Peel and core the apples and cut into bite-sized pieces. Peel and chop the onion.

Put the mangoes, apples and onion into a large saucepan with the remaining ingredients over a medium heat and bring to the boil. Reduce the heat and simmer, stirring occasionally, for about 45 minutes, until the chutney has thickened.

Remove from the heat and spoon into warm sterilised jars. Seal tightly and store until ready to use.

lime pickle

		ingredients	
very easy		6 limes	2 garlic cloves, chopped
		3 fresh green chillies, deseeded and chopped	1½ tbsp white malt vinegar
serves 4		2 tbsp salt	3 tbsp sugar
		3 tbsp chilli oil	2 tsp paprika
15 minutes + at least 6 days to marinate		2.5-cm/1-inch piece fresh root ginger, chopped	2 tsp mustard powder
			1 tsp garam masala
12–15 minutes			

Cut the limes into eighths and remove the pips. Squeeze some of the juice from each of the limes into a large, sterilised jar, then add the squeezed lime pieces and chillies. Sprinkle over half of the salt, cover tightly with a non-corrodible lid and shake well. Leave in a sunny place for at least 6 days, adding a teaspoon of salt every other day and shaking the jar at least once a day.

Heat the oil in a saucepan over a low heat, add the ginger and garlic and cook for 3 minutes. Pour in the vinegar, then add the lime and chilli mixture and any juices. Stir well and cook for 4 minutes. Add the sugar, paprika, mustard powder and garam masala and cook for a further 3 minutes.

Remove from the heat, spoon into sterilised jars and seal tightly. Store in a cool, dark place until ready to use.

index